Thirty-One Mysteries
to Solve

Clue by Clue

CONVERSATION ACTIVITIES

Walton Burns

PRO LINGUA ASSOCIATES

Pro Lingua Associates, Publishers

74 Cotton Mill Hill, Suite A 315

Brattleboro, Vermont 05301 USA

Office: 802-257-7779

Orders: 800-366-4775

Email: info@ProLinguaAssociates.com

WebStore: www.ProLinguaAssociates.com

SAN: 216-0579

*At Pro Lingua
our objective is to foster an approach
to learning and teaching that we call
interplay, the **inter**action of language
learners and teachers with their materials,
with the language and culture,
and with each other in active, creative,
and productive **play**.*

Clue by Clue was designed and set in Adobe Times New Roman by Arthur A. Burrows. This is a digital font based on an early twentieth century old-fashioned serif type called Times New Roman, commissioned by the British newspaper *The Times* in 1931 and designed by Victor Lardent for the Monotype company. Digitized and distributed with Microsoft products, it has become one of the most widely used typefaces in history. It is easy to read, with strong contrasting bold and italic faces.

The illustrations in this book are from the Dreamstime.com Agency. The front cover illustration is © Nadeika. The other spot illustrations used throughout the book first appear on the pages noted. They are, on the title page, by © A=papantoniou, on page 2 by © Jasperodus, and on page 3 by © Irokez.

The book was printed and bound by Royal Palm Press in Punta Gorda, Florida.

Printed in the United States of America

Second printing 2018.

CONTENTS

Introduction

Clue by Clue is a collection of short mysteries to be solved by intermediate level English languge learners as they proceed through a series of clues. It can be used from upper elementary school to adult ESL learners. Each mystery is formatted as a two-page activity. One page is for the teacher, the other a photocopyable page of clues. In addition to being a supplementary activity for speaking and listening practice, the challenge of solving the mystery also requires critical thinking skills.

Acknowledgements

To the English Club in Astana, Kazakhstan, who were the first to try these activities.

WB

User's Guide

What is *Clue by Clue*?

Clue by Clue is a conversation activity. Students are given a brief description of a crime or puzzle — a mystery to solve. The mystery may be to find out who did it. It may be to find out which suspect is lying, or what clue the police find suspicious. It may be to figure out how the criminal did it and got away with it. Students are then given clues to the crime, one at a time. They read the clue and discuss its significance, while trying to solve the mystery. Once all the clues are handed out, they are able to solve the mystery.

Why Use *Clue by Clue*?

The *Clue by Clue* mysteries make great warm-up activities, conversation class activities, fillers, or even time-killers for those last few minutes of class. They can even be used to introduce units on crime or the justice system such as Pro Lingua's *Verdicts*. The activities lend themselves to practicing specific grammar points in a communicative setting. The clues are also designed to encourage discussion. While students are solving the mysteries they are also developing their spoken language skills, such as:

— Speculation (with modal verbs): *She must have forgotten her keys, ... It could have been the butler ...*

— Opinion language: *I think ..., I'm positive ..., I'm not sure ...*

— Hedging: *It's possible ..., probably ..., maybe ..., it's not impossible...*

— Conclusions: *That means that ...*

— Emphasis: *No way! I really think ...*

— Hypotheticals: *What if ..., If he was (were) ... ,*

— Expectations: *So the solution should be ...*

Finally, *Clue by Clue* teaches critical reading and thinking skills. To solve the mystery, students must read closely for details, synthesize information from different sources, apply prior knowledge about the world, identify unreliable narrators, and evaluate the logic of different arguments.

How to Use *Clue by Clue*

The estimated time needed to solve the mysteries is from 20 to 40 minutes, with most of the mysteries needing about 30 minutes. The thirty-one mysteries are arranged from easiest and fastest to solve ("The Empty Bank," about 20 minutes) to more difficult and longest ("The Third Man," 40 minutes). However, solving the mystery can take more or less time than the estimate, depending on the nature of the student group trying to solve the mystery.

1. To prepare, make one copy of the Clues Page for each pair or small group of students. Cut out the clue boxes for each group and make a small stack, being careful to preserve the order.

2. To play, put the students in groups or pairs. Hand out the situation and read it to them as they read/listen along.

3. Give them 3-5 minutes to discuss what might have happened. In more advanced groups, students could begin talking about what information they would need to solve the mystery. They might even begin to predict what evidence there will be.

4. Give each group the first clue and let them read it. Alternatively, you could project the clues one by one on a class screen, or write them on the board.

5. Give each group time to speculate on the meaning of the clue and what they think happened, typically 3-6 minutes depending on the clue. Monitor the groups to help with comprehension and also to

gauge when the students have exhausted the new information. When necessary, you can remind the students how the new clue relates to older clues.

6. Hand out the second clue; again give them time to speculate on the clue and how their opinions may have changed.

7. If the students are having trouble, you can read them the hints on the Teacher Page.

8. Once they have gone through all the clues, have the students discuss all the evidence as a whole and come to a conclusion that solves the mystery.

9. Ask each group to give their solution to the mystery. Be sure to encourage the students to speak in detail. It's not enough for them to say they think Suspect One is guilty. They need to give reasons. As with many mysteries, there is often a short list of suspects, so guessing is easy.

10. When the students have finished stating their solution, read the solution on the teacher page. Ask the students how plausible they find the solution. They can also discuss any unanswered questions about the crime that aren't revealed in the story, such as speculating about a motive.

11. Some of the mysteries have follow-up questions. As time permits, read the questions and talk about them in groups or as a whole class.

12. A variation:

   a. To turn it into a competitive activity, place each group's stack at the front of the classroom. Once the students have read and understood the situation, tell them to come get the first clue.

   b. Tell the students that they can take the next clue after 3 minutes. This encourages students to think fast.

c. After three minutes, each group should send someone to get the next clue. Use a bell to signal the time.

d. Repeat this until every group has every clue.

e. Then give the students as much time as they need to solve the mystery. This rewards students who don't think as fast, but process information well. The first group to solve the mystery correctly, with a clear explanation of their logic, wins.

13. Other variations:

a. After a suspect has been identified, you could organize a sort of mock trial with suspect, defense team, prosecutors, judge, and witnesses.

b. Small groups could be a team of investigators conducting police investigation based on the evidence. They can interview the suspects.

A suggestion:

After cutting out the clues it is a good idea to paste them on index cards, and to give the cards a longer life, laminate them.

The Empty Bank

The Situation

In the middle of the night, ten police cars drive up to a bank and surround it. They begin calling for everyone in the bank to come out with their hands up. When no one answers, they enter the bank and discover there is no one inside. What has happened?

Hints

1. Did anyone leave the bank before the police came?

2. Did anyone leave the bank after the police came?

3. Why did the police think someone was in the bank?

4. Could they have made a mistake?

The Solution

The resident and the police saw an advertisement inside the bank. The advertisement was a cardboard cutout of a person, so they thought they saw a person. In fact, there was no one in the bank except for the cutout.

 Teacher Page

The Empty Bank

The Situation

In the middle of the night, ten police cars drive up to a bank and surround it. They begin calling for everyone in the bank to come out with their hands up. When no one answers, they enter the bank and discover there is no one inside. What has happened?

The Clues

1. A local resident passed by the bank at night and saw someone inside. She phoned the police.	2. When the police entered the bank, all alarms were on and working perfectly.
3. No one had tripped the alarms all night.	4. When the police arrived they also saw a figure inside the bank.
5. There is only one exit to the bank, and the police saw no one leave.	6. When police called for anyone in the bank to come out, the figure did not move.
7. In fact, the figure did not move at all the whole night.	

The Midnight Robbery

The Situation

Airplane pilot Joana Li leaves her hotel room in the middle of the night to go to the airport. She is robbed right outside the hotel. She gives the thief all her money. She then goes straight to the nearest police station. She can't describe the thief because he was wearing a mask. However, police find two suspects in the area. Which suspect did it?

Hints

1. When you hear the word Captain, what do you think of?

2. Do you think of a pilot?

3. Did the mugger know Joana Li was a pilot?

4. Which suspect knew she was a pilot?

The Solution

Suspect #2 is guilty. They asked him if he saw Captain Li today, and he knew she was an airplane pilot. Most people associate the word Captain with the military or possibly the head of a ship. Remember that the mugger saw her pilot's uniform. He even grabbed the gold wings on her jacket that symbolize flying.

Follow-Up Questions

1. Can you think of other jobs that might begin in the middle of the night?
2. Would you expect a woman to be an airplane pilot? Why or why not?
3. Are there some jobs that we associate only with men or women?
4. Is it fair to think there are some jobs a woman can't do?

 Teacher Page

The Midnight Robbery

The Situation

Airplane pilot Joana Li leaves her hotel room in the middle of the night to go to the airport. She is robbed right outside the hotel. She gives the thief all her money. She then goes straight to the nearest police station. She can't describe the thief, because he was wearing a mask. However, police find two suspects in the area. Which suspect did it?

The Clues

1. Suspect 1 was asked, "Did you mug anyone tonight?" He said, "No, of course not! You can search me. I don't have any money on me, so how could I have taken money from anyone?"	2. Suspect 2 was asked, "Did you see Captain Li tonight?" He said, "No, I don't know anything about an airline pilot. I didn't see her."
3. Captain Li told police the mugger was upset she had only $20 on her.	4. The robber pulled the gold wings off her uniform before running away. However, they are not really made of gold.

The Award Certificate

The Situation

A man is awarded a certificate for 20 years of service for the government. He never receives the certificate. In fact, he is fired two weeks after being sent the certificate. What happened?

Hints

1. Who did the man work with?

2. What proof is there that he went to work?

3. Why did he respond only to the letters sent to his home?

The Solution

The man had started skipping work. He was rarely seen at his office, and his office telephone was always busy. Because the man worked alone and he didn't have a lot of work, he started staying home instead of working!

Follow-Up Questions

1. This is based on a true story. Do you know any other stories of people avoiding work?
2. What's the funniest thing you've ever done to avoid work?

 Teacher Page

The Award Certificate

The Situation

A man is awarded a certificate for 20 years of service for the government. He never receives the certificate. In fact, he is fired two weeks after being sent the certificate. What happened?

The Clues

1. The award is given to everyone who has worked for the government for 20 years.	2. The man worked in a small regional office of the government department of health.
3. His job was to collect complaints about the department of health from local people.	4. Everyone in the village where he worked knew him well, but recently no one had gone to see him at the office.
5. He was the only person who worked in that office. The office was in an obscure location.	6. The certificate was mailed to his office. He never answered.
7. Two weeks after they sent the certificate, they called to ask if he had received the certificate. They couldn't reach him by phone at the office. The next day an inspector found the office door locked.	8. The letter notifying him that he was fired was sent to his home address.
	9. After he received the letter, he called to complain about being fired, but he was fired anyway.

The Fireplace Poker

The Situation

Mrs. Steinman is found dead on her living room rug. The police are sure her husband did it. How do they know?

Hints

1. What was the murder weapon?

2. How was Mrs. Steinman killed?

3. Would you expect the fireplace poker would be used to stab someone?

4. How did the husband know how his wife was killed?

The Solution

The husband saw the fireplace poker and knew that she had been stabbed with it. However, most people would assume that a poker was used to beat someone to death. The police took the body away before the husband arrived. The only way the husband could know she was stabbed was if he had done it.

 Teacher Page

The Fireplace Poker

The Situation

Mrs. Steinman is found dead on her living room rug. The police are sure her husband did it. How do they know?

The Clues

1. Mrs. Steinman's maid found her dead when she came to work at noon.	2. There was a bloody fireplace poker near her body.
3. She had a large messy, bloody hole in her chest.	4. Police believe she was stabbed by the fireplace poker.
5. Because her death was so awful, police waited until the body was removed before calling her husband at work.	6. As soon as the husband arrived, he saw the bloody poker and said, "Find whoever stabbed her and lock them up."

The Night Watchman

The Situation

At 9:30 Tuesday morning, Frank Malone, the night watchman for a warehouse, comes into his boss's office. He tells him he is worried that the boss will be killed. The boss fires Frank immediately. What did the watchman do wrong?

Hints

1. What is Frank Malone's job?

2. Why did he think the boss's life was in danger?

3. When do people usually have dreams?

The Solution

Frank is fired for sleeping on the job. He tells the boss that he had a bad dream the night before. That would be Monday night. But Frank is supposed to be working as night watchman. He shouldn't be sleeping at night.

Follow-Up Questions

1. Do you believe that people's dreams can come true?
2. Do you believe that some people can sense when bad things will happen?

 Teacher Page

The Night Watchman

The Situation

At 9:30 Tuesday morning, Frank Malone, the night watchman for a warehouse, comes into his boss's office. He tells him he is worried that the boss will be killed. The boss fires Frank immediately. What did the watchman do wrong?

The Clues

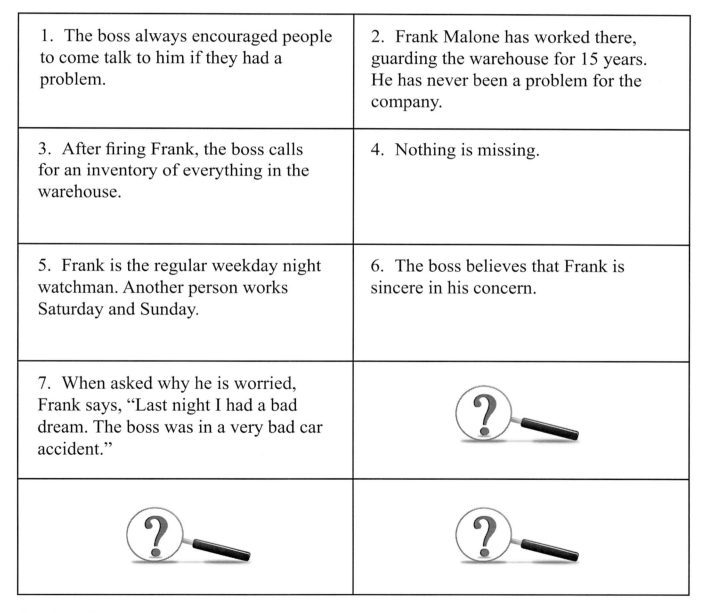

1. The boss always encouraged people to come talk to him if they had a problem.	2. Frank Malone has worked there, guarding the warehouse for 15 years. He has never been a problem for the company.
3. After firing Frank, the boss calls for an inventory of everything in the warehouse.	4. Nothing is missing.
5. Frank is the regular weekday night watchman. Another person works Saturday and Sunday.	6. The boss believes that Frank is sincere in his concern.
7. When asked why he is worried, Frank says, "Last night I had a bad dream. The boss was in a very bad car accident."	

The Mystery Mugger

The Situation

A man is mugged in an alley. The thief immediately runs away. The victim yells for the police, and a nearby officer comes within a few minutes. He is able to find two suspects close by who match the description of the thief. Both say they are innocent. Which one is lying?

Hints

1. What was the mugger wearing?

2. Is it possible that he really saw what he says he saw?

The Solution

The second suspect is lying. He said he saw someone running away. He didn't see his face, so he must have only seen his back. In that case, he wouldn't have seen the front of his T-shirt. So he wouldn't be able to say that the T-shirt had a superhero logo on the front.

Follow-Up Question

Do you think it is easy to remember the details of a crime, such as what the criminal looked like?

 Teacher Page

The Mystery Mugger

The Situation

A man is mugged in an alley. The thief immediately runs away. The victim yells for the police, and a nearby officer comes within a few minutes. He is able to find two suspects close by who match the description of the thief. Both say they are innocent. Which one is lying?

The Clues

1. The victim said the mugger pointed a gun at him and said, "Give me your wallet now!" He then ran off.	2. The victim described the mugger as having light eyes, dark hair, and a small nose. He was wearing jeans and a dark T-shirt with a superhero logo on the front.
3. Suspect one said, "I must have walked past that alley but I didn't go in. I was on my way to work. I work at the comic book store around the corner. That's why I'm wearing a superhero shirt."	4. Suspect two said, "I saw a guy running out of that alley. I didn't see his face because he was running away from me. But I remember his superhero T-shirt." It looked just like the other suspect's!"

The Courtyard of Death

The Situation

A woman falls to her death into the hotel courtyard from her hotel room window. While it looks like a suicide, police think someone pushed or threw her out the window. Why do they think so?

Hints

1. What did police have to do before they could test how Ms. Rosenthal fell?

2. Did Ms. Rosenthal close the window?

3. Had anyone been in the room since she died?

4. Who closed the window?

The Solution

Police found the window closed. If Ms. Rosenthal jumped, she couldn't have closed the window. Since the bed was still unmade and the room was still messy, it is unlikely that the hotel staff or anyone else had been in the room. But someone must have been in the room and closed the window. It was probably the same person who killed Ms. Rosenthal.

 Teacher Page

The Courtyard of Death

The Situation

A woman falls to her death into the hotel courtyard from her hotel room window. While it looks like a suicide, police think someone pushed or threw her out the window. Why do they think so?

The Clues

1. Police identified the body as Claire Rosenthal, a guest at the hotel.	2. They found the room with a Do Not Disturb Sign on the door. No one had cleaned the room that day.
3. Police found many fingerprints in the room. It was impossible to tell if she had been alone.	4. The police tried to test if the body fell or was pushed by dropping a dummy out the window.
5. The test was inconclusive; it was possible she had jumped.	6. The ledge outside the window was only 6 inches wide.

The Stolen Letter Affair

The Situation

A man murders a woman named Jennifer Slocum. For the next three days he checks the mailbox of a woman named Sarah Smith. On the third day he steals a letter from her box. Why does he do this?

Hints

1. Why did the man kill Jennifer instead of just leaving her?

2. Who sent the letter that the man stole?

3. What was in the letter the man stole?

4. Who was supposed to get that letter?

5. How long does it take for a letter to be mailed and delivered?

The Solution

Jennifer wanted to send proof of the affair to the man's wife. However, she didn't know her address. She looked the address up in the phone book. There was only one Sarah Smith in the phone book. She sent the letter to this Sarah Smith, not the man's wife.

The man killed Jennifer to stop her from telling his wife. Then he waited for her letter about the affair to come to his home. He got the mail at his home before his wife could see the letter. However, he also looked in the phone book and realized there was another Sarah Smith in town, and went to her house to check the mail just in case the letter came there.

Follow-Up Questions

1. Have you ever met someone with your name?
2. Have you ever seen a profile online that was similar to yours or someone you know?
3. Have you ever contacted someone only to find out it wasn't the person you thought it was?

 Teacher Page

The Stolen Letter Affair

The Situation

A man murders a woman named Jennifer Slocum. For the next three days he checks the mailbox of a woman named Sarah Smith. On the third day he steals a letter from her box. Why does he do this?

The Clues

1. The man's wife was also named Sarah Smith.	2. The man burned the letter he stole without opening it.
3. For three days, the man checked their own mail before his wife could.	4. A Sarah Smith is listed in the phone book at 27 Spruce Street.
5. The man and his wife live at Highlawn Court. They are not listed in the phone book.	6. The man was cheating on his wife with Jennifer Slocum.
7. Jennifer Slocum wanted the man to leave his wife and marry her.	8. The day that she died, Jennifer told the man that she had mailed his wife proof of their affair.

The Switched Signs

The Situation

A man who lives at 59 Church Street in Eden, Wisconsin goes out at 8:00 p.m. and takes down the street sign on his street, Church Street. He switches it with the street sign of the next street over, Elm Street. The next morning, he goes for an early walk and switches them back. Why did he do this?

Hints

1. What is the man's address?

2. What happened at 59 Elm Street?

3. Why did the killer have trouble finding the man?

4. Why didn't the killer use GPS?

The Solution

The man was tipped off that the gang was planning to kill him. He also knew that the gang would rely on maps instead of GPS. He also knew that both his street and Elm Street were next to each other. Both were streets with houses and no stores. And there is a 59 Elm Street. Because both streets are so similar, he hoped it would confuse the hit man. He was correct. The hit man went to the wrong street and killed the wrong person.

Follow-Up Questions

1. A lot of books and movies show innocent people getting caught up with organized crime. Do you think this is something that happens in real life?
2. Do you believe this man's plan would work in real life?
3. Do you rely on GPS or navigation websites? Do you ever look at a map and plan your own trip?
4. Do you think some day people will rely on GPS so much that they won't even know where they are?

 Teacher Page

The Switched Signs

The Situation

    A man who lives at 59 Church Street in Eden, Wisconsin goes out at 8:00 p.m. and takes down the street sign on his street, Church Street. He switches it with the street sign of the next street over, Elm Street. The next morning, he goes for an early walk and switches them back. Why did he do this?

The Clues

1. Both Church Street and Elm Street are dead-end streets that start from East Main Street.	2. Both streets are lined with houses.
3. The man worked as an accountant.	4. After the man switched the signs, someone was murdered that night at 59 Elm Street.
5. A few months ago, he quit his job and he was hired by a criminal gang who offered him a lot of money to work for them.	6. The man was recently approached by the police to help them collect evidence against the criminal gang.
7. The man had once overheard the leader of the gang order his men to never use GPS. The leader said it could leave a history of where they went.	8. The man got a phone call at 6:00 p.m. from a member of the gang who liked him, saying the gang knew he was talking to the police, and they were coming to "get" him tomorrow.

The Key Clue

The Situation

Veronica Horn broke both her legs while mountain climbing. She cannot leave her house while they heal. Because she lives alone, she starts getting everything delivered to the house. On Friday morning, her mailman finds her dead. He immediately calls the police and tells them exactly who did it. Who did it, and how does the mailman know?

Hints

1. What day was she killed on?

2. Who has come to her house in the past week?

3. Is there anything that should be on her front doorstep, but isn't?

The Solution

The newspaper delivery man did it. Veronica died on Tuesday, but the last newspaper at the front door was delivered on Monday. The newspaper delivery person didn't deliver to her on Tuesday, Wednesday, Thursday, and Friday, because he knew she was dead. Since her groceries were still out along with the package, it's unlikely that Veronica took the other papers in and forgot Monday's newspaper. Apparently the killer forgot to retrieve Monday's paper after he killed her.

Follow-Up Question

Have you ever been stuck at home alone for a long time? What did you do for fun?

 Teacher Page

The Key Clue

The Situation

    Veronica Horn broke both her legs while mountain climbing. She cannot leave her house while they heal. Because she lives alone, she starts getting everything delivered to the house. On Friday morning, her mailman finds her dead. He immediately calls the police and tells them exactly who did it. Who did it, and how does the mailman know?

The Clues

1. Veronica Horn traveled a lot, so she had few close friends in town.	2. She broke her legs while climbing Mount Kilimanjaro with a tour group.
3. The mailman had started bringing the mail in, because of her limited mobility, and to give her some company. She liked the visits because she was lonely.	4. Veronica didn't get any mail on Wednesday or Thursday, but on Friday morning, when the mailman rang the doorbell, Veronica didn't answer. He opened the unlocked door. He saw her dead body and immediately dialed 911.
5. Police said she had been dead a few days, but they couldn't say exactly how many.	6. The mailman said something he saw on the doorstep made him suspicious of one particular person.
7. On the doorstep was that morning's grocery delivery, a package with some new clothes, and Monday's newspaper.	

The Suspicious Suicide

The Situation

Benjamin Aman is found dead in his office. He was speaking on the phone to his lawyer when he was shot. The lawyer heard the gunshot. The lawyer also says he heard Benjamin talking to someone in the room. But with no proof, the police can do nothing. What proof is there that Benjamin was killed?

Hints

1. What was Benjamin doing when he was killed?

2. What happened to the phone after he died?

3. Who used the phone after Benjamin?

4. What did they have to do to use the phone?

The Solution

The proof that someone killed Benjamin is that the phone was hung up after he died. Benjamin was on the phone when he died. But the assistant had to pick the phone up to call the police. That means someone hung up the phone after Benjamin died.

Follow-Up Question

Many mysteries involve a businessman killing himself or being killed over a business deal. How common do you think that really is?

 Teacher Page

The Suspicious Suicide

The Situation

Benjamin Aman is found dead in his office. He was speaking on the phone to his lawyer when he was shot. The lawyer heard the gunshot. The lawyer also says he heard Benjamin talking to someone in the room. But with no proof, the police can do nothing. What proof is there that Benjamin was killed?

The Clues

1. The police found the gun in Benjamin's hands with only his fingerprints on it.	2. Benjamin was in danger of being sued over problems with his business. He called his lawyer to find out how serious the situation was.
3. According to his lawyer, Benjamin would probably have been forced to go out of business, which would have left him bankrupt.	4. His lawyer says that as they were talking, Benjamin dropped the phone and said, "Please, don't do this." Then he heard a gunshot.
5. The lawyer hung up and called the police, but it took him a few minutes because the lawyer lives in Florida and he had to find the number for the New York City police.	6. Before the police could get there, Benjamin's assistant came in and found him dead.
	7. The assistant said that he immediately took the phone off the hook and called the police.

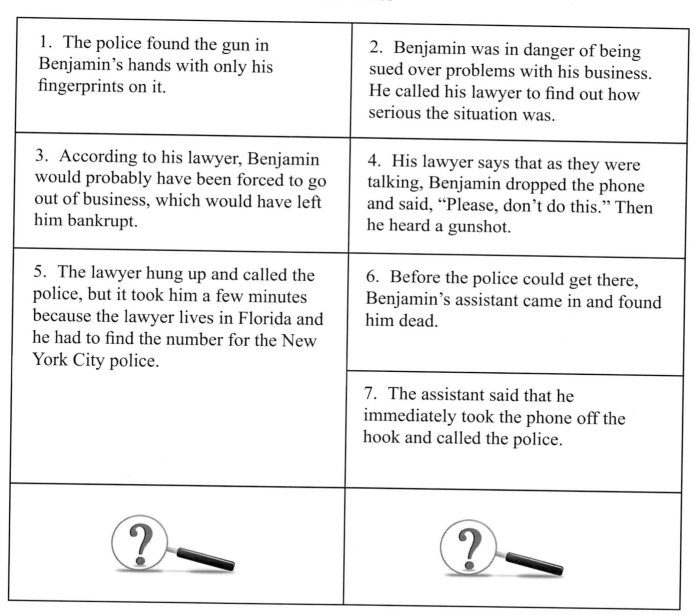

The Drive-Through Drama

The Situation

A man stops at a fast-food restaurant drive-through window to order food. However, the restaurant refuses to serve him. Why?

Hints

1. How did the man get to the restaurant?

2. Why do you think he was in danger?

3. Why would he be slower than other customers?

The Solution

The man was not in a car. He walked through the drive-through lane, which is for cars only. The restaurant was worried that a car could hit him in the drive-through lane.

Follow-Up Question

What are some funny things you could do in a drive-through?

 Teacher Page

The Drive-Through Drama

The Situation

A man stops at a fast-food restaurant drive-through window to order food. However, the restaurant refuses to serve him. Why?

The Clues

1. The man came at around 7 p.m. to order dinner.	2. He ordered a hamburger, French fries, and a soda.
3. The man had no special diet requests.	4. He spoke in a clear and easy-to-understand voice.
5. The restaurant took his order as usual and only refused him service when he came around to the window to get his food.	6. When the restaurant worker saw him, she insisted that he come into the restaurant to be served.
7. The man was very angry and called the police, claiming his rights were violated.	8. The man told police, "I'm working late next door. I wanted a quick dinner. So I walked over here and I didn't want to waste time going into the restaurant."
9. The restaurant said they insisted he come in because safety regulations did not allow walk-ups.	

The Poisoned Drink

The Situation

Magrit Zell is a secret agent for Uzakistan. She recently uncovered a ring of spies from Burakia. While on vacation on the Uzakistani coast, she meets a very interesting person named Natalya Hale. Ms. Hale, is a Burakian secret agent. She invites Ms. Zell to have drinks at Ms. Hale's beachfront home. Ms.Zell is a little suspicious of Ms. Hale, but she seems to be simply looking for friendship. Despite taking precautions, Ms. Zell is poisoned to death. How did Ms. Hale do it?

Hints

1. Besides water, what else was in Ms. Zell's glass?

2. What happens to drinks when the weather is hot?

3. Can you make ice cubes out of things other than water?

The Solution

Natalya Hale poisoned the water she used to make the ice cubes. She drank her drink while the poison was still frozen. However, after an hour or two in the hot sun, the ice would have melted and the poison entered the drink. Ms. Zell kept drinking, while Ms. Hale stopped drinking before that point.

Follow-Up Questions

1. Can you think of any other clever ways to poison someone?
2. What are some other interesting things you could put in ice?

 Teacher Page

The Poisoned Drink

The Situation

Magrit Zell is a secret agent for Uzakistan. She recently uncovered a ring of spies from Burakia. While on vacation on the Uzakistani coast, she meets a very interesting person named Natalya Hale. Ms. Hale is a Burakian secret agent. She invites Ms. Zell to have drinks at Ms. Hale's beachfront home. Ms. Zell is a little suspicious of Ms. Hale, but she seems to be simply looking for friendship. Despite taking precautions, Ms. Zell is poisoned to death. How did Ms. Hale do it?

The Clues

1. Both women had a glass of Bourbon whiskey on the rocks. They also had a large tray of snacks, including cheese, olives, breadsticks, and olive oil dip.	2. The two women talked for about two hours on the veranda overlooking the beach and the people swimming.
3. Ms. Hale drank her whiskey quite fast, and then had a second glass without ice.	4. Ms. Zell left Ms. Hale's house around 3:00 p.m.; and by 4:00 p.m. she was dead.
5. Doctors said she probably ingested the poison around 2:00 p.m.	6. After Ms. Zell left, Ms. Hale cleaned her freezer very thoroughly.

The Locked Room

The Situation

The president of Trojan Bank, George Wentworth, arrives at 7:15 every morning, usually before anyone else. He gets his coffee and then goes into his office to study the daily briefings from the department and branch managers. He always locks his door and his secretary knows not to disturb him until he comes out later in the morning.

On Tuesday, he is found dead in his office. Heart attack? Suicide? After investigating, the police believe he was murdered. Why do they think so?

Hints

1. Who was in the office break room with Wentworth?

2. If the president poisoned himself, where is the poison container?

3. If the police suspect murder, who are the suspects?

4. Which suspect is probably the murderer? How can you prove it?

The Solution

There is no doubt that the president died of poisoning. Although it is possible the president was depressed and became suicidal, the fact that he angrily fired a branch manager suggests that in the face of failure, he would fight to make things right. But how did he poison get into the coffee? In the morning whoever was in the office break room, could have put the poison into the coffee when the president took the reports into his office. There is no mention of finding a poison container so it is unlikely that the president poisoned his own coffee when he returned to his office. Murder is suspected, but who are the suspects? Further investigation is needed.

 Teacher Page

The Locked Room

The Situation

The president of Trojan Bank, George Wentworth, arrives at 7:15 every morning, usually before anyone else. He gets his coffee and then goes into his office to study the daily briefings from the department and branch managers. He always locks his door and his secretary knows not to disturb him until he comes out later in the morning.

On Tuesday, he is found dead in his office. Heart attack? Suicide? After investigating, the police believe he was murdered. Why do they think so?

The Clues

1. Recently the reports have not been good. The bank is in trouble.	2. A courier brings the reports at 7:30. He tells the police Wentworth was in the office break room making a pot of coffee and talking with someone.
3. Wentworth comes out of the office break room, and takes the reports into his office.	4. He comes back to get his coffee, thanks the courier, and offers him a cup of coffee. The courier says, " No, thanks."
5. Wentworth's secretary arrives as usual at 8:00 a.m. and finds nothing amiss. She makes a fresh pot of coffee.	6. The vice-president for investments recently made some very bad decisions. They will probably show up in today's reports.
7. Yesterday, the president angrily fired a branch manager whose branch was losing money.	8. At 10:00 a.m. the secretary tries to call Wentworth. He doesn't answer. She knocks on the door. No response. She calls maintenance and they get the door open.
9. Wentworth is slumped in his chair. The reports and his coffee mug are on the floor.	10. The police lab technician finds traces of a deadly poison in the coffee.

The Art Thief

The Situation

Blake Hamilton is a well-known art thief. He is arrested for stealing the famous painting, "Apple Trees in Summer" from the City Museum. Even though police find the painting in his apartment, he is never convicted for the crime. Why not?

Hints

1. Who needed to get rid of the search warrant?

2. What was the warrant made of?

3. Is that something easy to get rid of?

The Solution

When the police weren't looking, Blake destroyed the search warrant. The judge didn't have another copy. That means police cannot prove they had the right to search his apartment. According to the law, that means they cannot use anything they found in his apartment to prove he did the crime. Since Blake's father is a lawyer, Blake would have been well aware of police procedure in this matter.

Follow-Up Questions

1. Do you think this story is believable?
2. Do you think police should be able to break rules when they have proof of a crime?

 Teacher Page

The Art Thief

<table>
<tr><td colspan="2">

The Situation

Blake Hamilton is a well-known art thief. He is arrested for stealing the famous painting, "Apple Trees in Summer" from the City Museum. Even though police find the painting in his apartment, he is never convicted for the crime. Why not?
</td></tr>
</table>

The Clues

1. Security cameras in the museum clearly showed Blake stealing the painting.	2. The painting in Blake's apartment was verified as real by an art expert.
3. Police identified Blake quickly from the security cameras, but it took them two days to find out where he lived.	4. They discovered his address by tracing a phone call he made in the middle of the night to his father, a well-known lawyer.
5. As soon as they got his address, they called a judge to get a search warrant. Because it was the middle of the night, they had to go to the judge's house.	6. The judge had no access to his work computer or files at home, so he wrote the warrant out on an ordinary piece of paper.
7. Police got to Blake's house at 2:00 a.m. He immediately demanded to see the warrant, which they gave to him.	8. Police found the painting in the ceiling of a closet in a small bedroom at the back of the apartment.
9. The police left without the search warrant.	

The Secret Recipe

The Situation

Paul Romano is the son of the owner of a famous Italian restaurant, Romano's Italian Café. Paul Romano is found dead. Who killed him and why?

Hints

1. Why did Paul Romano look at the secret recipe?

2. Did he give the recipe to anyone?

3. Did the recipe help those people?

4. How does the head chef know the recipe to the sauces?

The Solution

Antony Viglione killed Paul Romano for giving him a bad recipe. The recipe was kept in a safe. Paul Romano took it out and copied it. He sold it to Viglione's so they could compete with Romano's Italian Café. Unfortunately, the secret recipe was a fake. It was just an advertising trick. The chef cooked the sauce from memory as he had learned it from Paul Romano's grandmother.

 Teacher Page

The Secret Recipe

The Situation

Paul Romano is the son of the owner of a famous Italian restaurant, Romano's Italian Café. Paul Romano is found dead. Who killed him and why?

The Clues

1. Romano's Italian Café is famous for its tomato sauce. The recipe is a traditional family recipe passed down through the Romano family.	2. Twenty years ago, Romano's Italian Café ran a series of ads about its secret recipe. They showed the recipe in a safe, guarded day and night.
3. Paul Romano was seen meeting with Antony Viglione, head chef of the gourmet restaurant, Viglione's.	4. Viglione's had recently started advertising its new and improved marinara sauce.
5. About six months ago, Paul Romano had opened the safe where the recipe is kept. No one had opened it for years before that.	6. Paul Romano was known for buying expensive cars, but his father didn't like this habit.
7. The chef at Romano's Italian Café had been a good friend of Paul Romano's grandmother, and learned the recipe from her.	8. The reviews of Viglione's Marinara Sauce were not good. Viglione's was not only embarrassed, they lost a lot of business.
9. The chef couldn't tell police who had written the recipe down. He himself had never read the recipe.	

The First Edition

The Situation

Kevin Hunt, a bookseller, goes to a rare book auction. He buys one item, an antique book, for $100,000. He takes it back to his bookstore and puts it on the shelves with the other books. A customer comes in later and buys it for $17.50. Why did the bookseller let this happen?

Hints

1. Where do you think the money in the bag came from?

2. Is the book really worth $100,000?

3. Which was more important, the book or giving money to the man who sold the book?

4. Does the man who sold the book now have a good explanation for the police where his money came from?

The Solution

Kevin Hunt is helping the criminal gang hide their illegally gained money. The gang gets money from drug deals. They give the money to Kevin. The gang controls the auctions. Kevin gives the money back to the gang by buying a book they are selling. Now the gang can say they get money from selling valuable books. This is called money-laundering.

The First Edition

The Situation

Kevin Hunt, a bookseller, goes to a rare book auction. He buys one item, an antique book, for $100,000. He takes it back to his bookstore and puts it on the shelves with the other books. A customer comes in later and buys it for $17.50. Why did the bookseller let this happen?

The Clues

1. The real value of the book is $15.00.	2. Two days before the auction, a man brought a bag of money to the bookseller.
3. The bag contained exactly $100,000.	4. The bag also contained a note with the title of the book.
5. The auction house that sold the book works with the man who brought the bag of money.	6. Both of them are known associates of a criminal gang that deals drugs.
7. Police have been trying to arrest the gang by investigating where the gang gets its money.	

The Prison Escape

The Situation

A man is being held in the police station jail. He escapes by walking out the front door. It takes hours for anyone to notice he is missing. How did he do it?

Hints

1. Did the policeman who was watching the video camera after the man escaped, see an empty cell or not?

2. What did the policeman watching the video camera see?

3. Why was the escape only discovered when he was seen in person?

4. Why did the man's brother wear an overcoat and a hat?

The Solution

The man and his brother switched clothes. The man walked out of the jail wearing the big hat and overcoat. The man's brother lay down to hide his face and pretended to sleep. The man watching through the camera wouldn't notice the difference. Brothers look enough alike that the police didn't recognize the man leaving the station was the prisoner. When the policeman came down to get the prisoner for dinner, however, he got a good look at the substitute's face.

 Teacher Page

The Prison Escape

The Situation

A man is being held in the police station jail. He escapes by walking out the front door. It takes hours for anyone to notice he is missing. How did he do it?

The Clues

1. The man escaped at 1:00 p.m. on an ordinary Friday in the summer.	2. The police station was operating as usual. There were staff members around.
3. The man had been arrested that morning for stealing a car. He was being held in jail until his court date on Monday morning.	4. The man did not pay any of the people at the station. He did not know any of the police working that day.
5. The police discovered he was missing at 7:00 p.m. when they went down to his cell to give him dinner.	6. The cell had a video camera in it that was watched at all times.
7. The policeman watching the video saw nothing unusual the whole day.	8. In the afternoon, the man lay down on the bed face first and napped.
9. The man was visited by his brother around 12:30.	10. The brother was wearing a large overcoat and a big hat.

The Lonely Victim

The Situation

A millionaire, Benjamin Huxley, is found dead in his study at home. He was shot in the head. A bullet also struck the clock behind him and broke it. The clock showed a time of death of about 10:00 a.m. However, no one else was home at 10:00 a.m. Security cameras show that only four people were at the house at all that morning:

- His wife, Sylvia Huxley

- His daughter, Sarah Huxley

- The family's housekeeper, Jane Turner

- Benjamin's assistant, Steven Browne

What happened, and who killed him?

Hints

1. Who would benefit directly from Mr. Huxley's death?

2. Who had access to Mr. Huxley between 8:00 and 9:00 a.m.?

3. Why did Sylvia ask Sarah to start the car? What is significant about the car?

4. Why is it so helpful that the clock was hit by a bullet?

The Solution

Sylvia, his wife, killed him. She was planning to leave him and she wanted to keep his money. No one would have checked on him during the day, because he liked to be alone in his study.

When Sylvia left the house, she went back inside. She waited until her daughter started the car and then walked into the study and shot her husband. She then set the clock at 10:03 and shot it. Finally she made a mess all around the area of the crime to make it look like there had been a struggle.

 Teacher Page

The Lonely Victim

The Situation

A millionaire, Benjamin Huxley, is found dead in his study at home. He was shot in the head. A bullet also struck the clock behind him and broke it. The clock showed a time of death of about 10:00 a.m. No one else was home at 10:00 a.m. Security cameras show that only four people were at the house at all that morning: his wife, Sylvia Huxley; his daughter, Sarah Huxley; the family's housekeeper, Jane Turner; and Benjamin's assistant, Steven Browne. What happened, and who killed him?

The Clues

1. Steven Browne, who found the body, came at 11:00 a.m. as usual. However, he didn't call the police until 11:45 a.m.	2. The area around Mr. Huxley's desk, where the stopped clock was, was very disturbed – table overturned, things all over the floor.
3. The housekeeper said that she heard a bedroom door open when she left Mr. Huxley's coffee outside the study door at 8:30 and then left to go shopping downtown.	4. The neighbors confirmed that someone had left in Sylvia's car a little after 9:00. The neighbor two doors down said, "Sylvia drove an old diesel car. Very loud when it started up. You could always hear it, even inside with the windows closed."
5. Mrs. Huxley and her daughter went to town to shop for a wedding dress for Sarah, who was to be married in three months. They were there from around 9:30 to 11:00.	6. Searching his emails, police found that Mr. Huxley suspected his wife was cheating on him.
7. Right before she left the house with her daughter, Sylvia Huxley went back into the house to get her phone.	8. She told her daughter to wait five minutes to let the sun warm the engine, then start the car and let it run for a bit.

The Missing Weapon

The Situation

Jack Finnegan kills his neighbor, Edward Murphy, in an argument over how to cook lamb on a barbecue grill. Police can't prove Finnegan did it because they can't find the murder weapon. How did he do it?

Hints

1. Name everything that was in the backyard.

2. Was there anything that was in the backyard and then disappeared?

3. Why is it significant that the leg of lamb was frozen?

The Solution

Mr. Finnegan used the frozen leg of lamb to kill Mr. Murphy. It was very large. Frozen meat is also very heavy and very hard. The police could not test the leg of lamb because Mr. Finnegan had cooked it. He clearly invented the story of the man in black with the hammer.

Follow-Up Questions

1. Is this the perfect crime?
2. Can you think of any other ways to kill someone and get away with it?

Photocopyable © 2017 Walton Burns : ProLingua Associates.com   Teacher Page

The Missing Weapon

The Situation

Jack Finnegan kills his neighbor, Edward Murphy, in an argument over how to cook lamb on a barbecue grill. Police can't prove Finnegan did it because they can't find the murder weapon. How did he do it?

The Clues

1. Police found Mr. Murphy dead in Mr. Finnegan's backyard. He had been hit with a large, heavy, blunt object.	2. Mr. Finnegan's family told police that Mr. Murphy came over when he saw Mr. Finnegan carrying a frozen leg of lamb outside.
3. One neighbor told police, "Mr. Murphy was yelling that it was crazy to grill lamb when it was still frozen."	4. Mr. Finnegan's family went inside to avoid the fight, as did the nearby neighbors.
5. Mr. Finnegan told police an insane man in black ran up with a hammer, hit Mr. Murphy on the head because he was making too much noise, and then ran away.	6. Police think Mr. Murphy was hit by something much larger than a hammer.
7. Nothing that looked like a murder weapon was found anywhere in the backyard.	8. The police tested everything they could find in Mr. Finnegan's house. Nothing they found could have been the weapon that killed Mr. Murphy.
9. Mr. Finnegan apologized to police that he had continued cooking the lamb while talking to them.	

The Jewelry Store Robbery

The Situation

John Young closes his jewelry store at 4 p.m. While he is putting the jewelry in the safe, a masked man comes in and takes all the jewels. Police find three suspects. Each one has an alibi, but one of them is lying. Which one is it?

- Frederick Cummins is a known jewel thief who lives a 10-minute walk from the store.

- Michael Kowalski has been seen standing outside the store at different times for the past week.

- Charles Lewis was a partner in the store when it first opened. John and Charles disagreed over the direction of business, sometimes arguing loudly in front of customers. Charles finally sold his shares in the store.

Hints

1. Who won the football game?

2. What did Frederick say about the football game?

The Solution

Frederick is lying. He said, "Go Giants," meaning he believes that the Giants won the football game. However, Michael says the Patriots won. The Giants were ahead until the last 10 minutes. Then the Patriots scored. Frederick didn't see that because he turned the game off early to make sure he made it to the jewelry store on time. Remember that it was important to be at the store by 4 p.m.

Follow-Up Questions

1. How often do you think jewelry stores get robbed?
2. Do you think it is easy to rob a jewelry store?
3. Sometimes we don't have any proof of where we are. If police asked you where you were last night, would you have a good alibi? What kind of proof would you have?

Teacher Page

The Jewelry Store Robbery

The Situation

John Young closes his jewelry store at 4:00 p.m. While he is putting the jewelry in the safe, a masked man comes in and takes all the jewels. Police find three suspects. Each one has an alibi, but one of them is lying. Which one is it? • Frederick Cummins is a known jewel thief who lives a 10-minute walk from the store. • Michael Kowalski has been seen standing outside the store at different times for the past week. • Charles Lewis was a partner in the store when it first opened. John and Charles disagreed over the direction of business, sometimes arguing loudly in front of customers. Charles finally sold his shares in the store.

The Clues

1. Frederick told police: "I know you guys think I'm a thief but you don't have any proof. Anyway, I couldn't have done it. I always watch football on Sunday afternoon. Yesterday the Giants played the Patriots. The game didn't end until 4:30. Go Giants!"

2. Michael told police: "I don't know anything about a jewelry store. Besides, I was watching the football game until about 4:20 or 4:30. It looked like the Giants were going to win. Then, the Patriots scored twice in the last ten minutes and won the game! Amazing!

3. Charles told police: "We disagreed about everything. Now I'm glad I sold my shares. I mean, who needs to go to work and fight every day? If you want to know where I was, I was home alone, reading a book."

4. John told police:"Whoever robbed the store knew what they were doing. The 10-20 minutes after closing is the best time to rob the store, before the jewels get put in the safe."

The Break-In

The Situation

Sasha Konstantinov, a successful businessman, is robbed. Everything of value is stolen. There are two suspects:

- his son, Mikhail Konstantinov, who was staying at the house

- Georges Fontaine, a well-known thief who was seen in the area.

Who did it?

Hints

1. Is there anything strange about Mikhail's story?

2. Why was there broken glass on the snow?

3. If you hit a glass window, which way does the broken glass go?

The Solution

Mikhail did it. He tried to make it look like someone had broken into the house. That's why he broke the window on the back door. However, police found glass outside the house. If you break a window from the outside, most of the glass will fall inside the house. The glass on the outside means that someone broke the window from the inside. That means Mikhail broke the window from inside.

Follow-Up Questions

1. They say that most crimes are committed by people known to the victims. Do you think that is true?
2. Have you ever heard any stories of people trying to make it look like someone else committed a crime?

 Teacher Page

The Break-In

The Situation

Sasha Konstantinov, a successful businessman, is robbed. Everything of value is stolen. There are two suspects: • his son Mikhail Konstantinov, who was staying at the house • Georges Fontaine, a well-known thief who was seen in the area. Who did it?

The Clues

1. Sasha Konstantinov's home in Greenwich, Connecticut, was broken into while he was away on a business trip.	2. His son, Mikhail, is the only other person who lives in the house.
3. Mikhail had large gambling debts. His father gave him no money, although he let him live in the house for free.	4. Police found a broken window on the back door.
5. Although the house had a security system, no alarms went off that day.	6. Georges Fontaine arrived in Greenwich on the same day that Sasha left. He had a ticket to leave the day after the robbery.
7. He refused to tell police why he came to Greenwich.	8. Georges has never been caught because of his careful planning and skill in disabling security systems.
9. When the police questioned Mikhail, he said, "Look at all this broken glass on the snow out here! Why would I break the door when I could just open it with a key?"	

The Bride's Missing Jewels

The Situation

Mary Johansen is getting dressed for her wedding in the basement of the church. She is planning to wear some very valuable jewelry. She leaves the room for a minute to use the bathroom. When she returns, all her jewelry is gone. Only the maintenance man and the gardener have no alibi. Who did it?

Hints

1. Why couldn't the gardener see clearly what was going on in the study?

2. What does he say he did to see better?

3. What happens when glass fogs up in the winter, and then what happens?

The Solution

The gardener. He is lying about seeing the maintenance man. He says that he brushed frost off the door. However, when it is cold outside, frost appears inside the window and not outside. He must have been lying.

The Bride's Missing Jewels

The Situation

Mary Johansen is getting dressed for her wedding in the basement of the church. She is planning to wear some very valuable jewelry. She leaves the room for a minute to use the bathroom. When she returns, all her jewelry is gone. Only the maintenance man and the gardener have no alibi. Who did it?

The Clues

1. Mary arrived at the church at 9 a.m. on a cold February morning. She had plenty of time to change into her wedding dress for her wedding at 11 a.m.	2. Her family was in the main hall of the church with the minister. The groom had not arrived, nor had any guests.
3. The gardener was shoveling snow outside the basement door.	4. The maintenance man was checking the heating system in the basement.
5. The heating system is located in a small room between the minister's study and the bathroom.	6. Brides always change in the minister's study, a comfortable room in the basement of the church.
7. At 10 a.m., Mary left the study to go to the bathroom at the other end of the hall. She returned 15 minutes later to find the jewels gone and the gardener inside the basement.	8. The maintenance man said he didn't leave the room with the heating system. No one saw him there. The bride doesn't remember hearing him either.
9. The gardener says the maintenance man probably stole the jewelry. He said he heard a noise, brushed the frost off the basement door window, and saw someone leaving the study.	

The Missing Money

The Situation

Mr. Fulton never trusted banks. Instead, he kept his money in a safe at home. When he was diagnosed with cancer, he told his son that he had saved up one million dollars. He said that his son would know where to find the money. However, after he died, his son finds the safe empty. Where is the money?

Hints

1. What did he and his son have in common?

2. What was the uniform of the singing group?

3. Did Mr. Fulton buy everything he needed?

The Solution

On Mr. Fulton's cufflinks were two valuable diamonds. That's why they were colorless and not green as they were supposed to be. Because he didn't trust banks and was scared of being robbed, he hid his money where no one would think to look for it, on a pair of cufflinks kept with his funeral clothes at a funeral home. He knew his son would be able to spot the difference because he had been in the singing group and would know the uniform well.

Follow-Up Questions

1. What has been the happiest time in your life so far?
2. Do you ever have nostalgia for the past?
3. Should parents encourage their children to do the same things they did?

 Teacher Page

The Missing Money

The Situation

Mr. Fulton never trusted banks. Instead, he kept his money in a safe at home. When he was diagnosed with cancer, he told his son that he had saved up one million dollars. He said that his son would know where to find the money. However, after he died, his son finds the safe empty. Where is the money?

The Clues

1. Nothing of value was found anywhere in the house or at his place of work.	2. No secret hiding places were found either.
3. The only thing of interest he bought before he died was the clothes he wanted to be buried in.	4. Those clothes were very odd. Mr. Fulton wanted to be buried in the uniform of his college singing group, the Rainbows. The uniform was famous for its bright colors: a bright purple suit coat, a red shirt, and cufflinks with green gemstones, an orange tie, yellow pants, and blue shoes.
5. Mr. Fulton thought his time singing with the Rainbows was the happiest time of his life. He was very happy when his son went to the same college and also sang in the Rainbows.	
	6. The funeral director thought the outfit was strange, but he agreed to keep the purple jacket, red shirt, cufflinks with clear gem stones, orange tie, yellow pants, and blue shoes until Mr. Fulton died.
7. A day before the funeral, the son visited the funeral home. He was surprised to see his father laid out in the Rainbow clothes. The funeral director said that Mr. Fulton had brought the entire costume to him for safekeeping a few weeks after he was diagnosed with cancer.	

The Unopened Letters

The Situation

A man mails himself two letters. When he receives the letters, he throws them away without opening them. Why does he do this?

Hints

1. Why was the man hired at his new job?

2. How long did the letters take to arrive?

3. Was that a problem?

4. What kind of problem did the man find?

5. Where do you think the man works?

The Solution

The man's new job was as head of the National Post Office. The regional post offices had problems delivering mail promptly. He sent the letters to himself to test how long it would take to get them. Obviously because of the results, he was very disappointed.

Follow-Up Questions

1. Do you think this is a good way to test the postal system?
2. Can you think of other ways a boss could test his company?

 Teacher Page

The Unopened Letters

<table>
<tr><td colspan="2">

The Situation

A man mails himself two letters. When he receives the letters, he throws them away without opening them. Why does he do this?

</td></tr>
</table>

The Clues

1. The man had recently gotten a new job.	2. The new job required him to move to the capital of his country.
3. The man had been hired to fix serious problems at his new place of work.	4. On his way to the capital, he stopped at two cities. In each city, he put one of the letters in a post office mailbox.
5. Both letters were addressed to his new home in the capital.	6. Both letters contained one blank piece of paper.
7. The piece of paper was ordinary white paper that he bought in a stationery store.	8. The first city was a two-day drive north of the capital city. The second city was one day's drive east of the capital city.
9. Both letters took five days to arrive.	10. The day after the letters came, he called a meeting with all the regional managers and was very angry with them. He told them that some things would have to change or else.

The Fake Map

The Situation

A man buys a high-quality reproduction of an old map. A friend sees the map and is impressed with the quality of the map. He suggests that the man get it tested to see if it is the original. The man agrees just for fun, and discovers that it is in fact the original. How did he get the original map?

Hints

1. How do the artists usually practice their work?

2. Is there any way the artist could have practiced with the original map?

3. Does anything indicate that he might have seen the original map lately?

4. Could the thief have accidentally returned a copy of the map?

The Solution

An artist who works for a publishing company stole the original map two months ago after the university refused to lend it to the company. He practiced for a week and then returned the map, but at that time he had gotten so good, he accidentally returned a copy instead of the original. He then secretly and accidentally sold the original.

Follow-Up Question

Do you like to see original documents or paintings, or are copies just as good?

The Fake Map

The Situation

A man buys a high-quality reproduction of an old map. A friend sees the map and is impressed with the quality of the map. He suggests that the man get it tested to see if it is the original. The man agrees just for fun, and discovers that it is in fact the original. How did he get the original map?

The Clues

1. The man immediately called the university where the original should have been. The university had their copy tested and found that it was not the original.	2. The man bought it from a publishing company that is famous for their copies of historical documents. They use the same materials as the original creators, and they do not mark their copies in any way.
3. The university told police that their copy had been stolen three months ago. It was returned a week later with a note saying, "Sorry."	4. They never reported it to police and never thought to test the map that was returned.
5. The owner of the publishing company told police that the artist who made that map was extremely good at copying original documents.	6. The owner said he couldn't even tell the artist's copies from the original.
7. The owner told police that they usually tried to borrow original documents and practice copying them.	8. He said the university didn't let them borrow the original map, for some reason.
9. They put in the request about three months ago.	

The Boss' Birthday

The Situation

The CEO of a large company turns 50. For his birthday, he decides to invite four employees to his house for dinner. Finally the four are chosen:

1. Joe Henderson from the Accounting Department

2. Jennifer Zhang from IT

3. Justine Saltzman from the Legal Department

4. David Houlihan, a sales person.

At dinner, all is going well until one of the boss' small figurines is found missing. Who took it?

Hints

1. Was the missing figurine easy to steal or hard?

2. Did the thief think anyone would notice the missing statue?

3. Why would David's present be unwrapped instead of carefully wrapped in a box and paper?

4. Why did David ask to see the Chinese art?

The Solution

David stole the statue. He had not thought to get the boss a gift. So, he had to improvise. He hoped the boss had enough art that he wouldn't recognize his own figurine. And he took one that was hard to see, hoping no one would notice. After the party, however, the maid told the boss one figurine was missing. That's why the boss recognized it as David's gift the minute he saw it.

 Teacher Page

The Boss' Birthday

The Situation

The CEO of a large company turns 50. For his birthday, he decides to invite four employees to his house for dinner. Finally the four are chosen:

1. Joe Henderson from the Accounting Department 2. Jennifer Zhang from IT
3. Justine Saltzman from the Legal Department 4. David Houlihan, a sales person.

At dinner, all is going well until one of his small figurines is found missing. Who took it?

The Clues

1. The four employees were picked up at their homes by a limousine and traveled together. On the way, they discussed the presents they had bought for their boss.	2. Joe had bought a very expensive gift, which made the others anxious that their gifts weren't good enough.
3. Jennifer had painted a handmade reproduction of a famous Chinese painting. The others were impressed by her talent at copying the artwork.	4. They were also surprised to learn about the boss' love of Chinese art—Jennifer knew only because he had mentioned it once, due to her Chinese ancestry.
5. David said only that he thought the boss would really like his present. It was in his pocket, but he hadn't had time to wrap it.	6. When they arrived, Justine tried to give the boss her gift. However, David quickly interrupted by asking to see the Chinese art collection.
7. After viewing the room with the art collection, the four left their presents on a table in the art collection room. They then went to dinner.	8. David's unwrapped present was a small ceramic figurine.
9. Seeing them go into the collection reminded the maid she hadn't cleaned it that week. Worried that the boss might be angry about that, she went in to clean after they left.	

The Missing Manuscript

The Situation

Jon Worthington, author of the very successful *Wizard World* series of books for young adults, spends all day Wednesday at the publishing house making the final changes on the only copy of the manuscript of his newest book. The publisher tells him that when he is finished he is to put the final copy in the safe and close it. On Thursday morning, the publisher comes to work and finds her office broken into and wrecked. And there is only blank paper in the safe.

Hints

1. Who was the last person to actually touch the manuscript?

2. Did that person have a motive to get rid of it?

3. Is there proof that anyone actually broke into the safe?

The Solution

Jon Worthington never put the manuscript back in the safe. When everyone went for lunch, he took paper from the printer next to his desk. At the end of the day, he put that paper in the safe and put the manuscript in his bag. Jon was not only tired of writing *Wizard World* books, he was very unhappy with his last effort. He did not want it published because he was afraid it would get very bad reviews. In addition, he wanted to do another project, and he wanted to get away from the *Wizard World* books. So he stole the copy, hoping that the publisher would not insist that he recreate the book, and that would be the end of the series. Then he could do more serious writing.

 Teacher Page

The Missing Manuscript

The Situation

Jon Worthington, author of the very successful *Wizard World* series of books for young adults, spends all day Wednesday at the publishing house making the final changes on the only copy of the manuscript of his newest book. The publisher tells him that when he is finished he is to put the final copy in the safe and close it. Thursday morning, the publisher comes to work and finds her office broken into and wrecked. And there is only blank paper in the safe.

The Clues

1. Only the publisher and the publisher's assistant had the combination to the safe.	2. The seven other *Wizard World* books were worth $15 million a year. Because of potential leaks, once the final manuscript was finished by the author, all other paper copies were destroyed.
3. The manuscript was kept in the publisher's office. All editing was done there too.	4. On Wednesday, Jon Worthington had been rewriting the digital copy, using the editor's notes on the paper manuscript. He worked all day long, even skipping lunch. Even so, he was very unhappy with his efforts.
5. He closed the safe himself around 6:00 p.m.	6. The publisher's assistant stayed at work until around 8:00 p.m., but says he didn't see or hear anything.
7. The woman who worked next to Jon's computer found her printer empty of paper on Thursday morning.	8. Recently in an interview Jon had said he wanted to write books that would be more important than *Wizard World*.

The Perfect Alibi

The Situation

After losing a billion-dollar contract to her rival NB Consulting, the CEO of Stone Consultants, Sonya Stone, sends a letter to Nora Bergstrom, President of NB Consulting. It says, "On December 22nd you will die."

On December 22nd, Ms. Bergstrom was on the phone with a friend until 8:00 p.m. Later that night she is indeed found dead. The letter was found on a coffee table. But Ms. Stone was seen by all her employees at a Christmas party that same night. How did Sonya Stone kill Nora Bergstrom?

Hints

1. Why did Sonya go back to Nevada every year?

2. Who did the security cameras see?

The Solution

Sonya had a twin sister. No one knew about her sister because they had no living parents or family, and because the orphanage burned down, leaving no records. While Sonya was giving her speech at the Christmas party, Sonya's twin went to Nora's apartment and shot her.

 Teacher Page

The Perfect Alibi

The Situation

After losing a billion-dollar contract to her rival NB Consulting, the CEO of Stone Consultants, Sonya Stone, sends a letter to Nora Bergstrom, President of NB Consulting. It says, "On December 22nd you will die."

On December 22nd, Ms. Bergstrom was on the phone with a friend until 8:00 p.m. Later that night she is indeed found dead. The letter was found on a coffee table. But Ms. Stone was seen by all her employees at a Christmas party that same night. How did Sonya Stone kill Nora Bergstrom?

The Clues

1. Nora Bergstrom was found shot to death in her apartment at 8:37pm.	2. Security cameras show a figure that looks like Sonya Stone entering Nora's apartment at around 8:15. The figure pulled out a gun and shot Nora and then left.
3. Sonya Stone's Christmas party started at 6 p.m. and went until midnight.	4. At 8:15 p.m. Sonya asked everyone to be silent while she gave a speech about the successes of the company. The speech was 30 minutes long, and several people videotaped it.
5. The Christmas party was held at the restaurant Chez Nous, which is on the other side of the city from Nora's apartment.	6. Sonya grew up as an orphan with no family in a small town in Nevada. She says that her difficult childhood helped her learn how to work hard.
7. The orphanage burned down years ago. However, Sonya often flies to Nevada.	8. Her last trip was on the 17th of December of this year.
9. She always visits the house of a woman in Nevada who has the exact same birthday, hair color, and height as Sonya.	

The Buried Coin

The Situation

In the middle of the night, someone digs up a grave in a cemetery. The caretaker of the cemetery lives nearby and hears the noise. The thief is surprised and runs away, not realizing he has dropped a coin that was worth $7 million. How did the coin get there?

Hints

1. Who knew about the coin?

2. Who had a chance to take the coin?

3. What was the chauffeur doing when Lucy came?

The Solution

The chauffeur stole the coin and put it in John Leigh's clothing. He would have known about the coin and probably saw where Frank kept it. When he heard that Frank was dead, he took it. When he saw Lucy coming down the hall, he realized she would notice it missing and that he might be searched. So he hid it in the clothes of a patient in the next room who had also died—in this case John Leigh. He then went and dug him up to steal the coin.

Follow-Up Questions

1. Do you have a lucky item that you carry around with you?
2. If you had a coin or jewel worth a lot of money, would you keep it with you?
3. Do you think it's possible for a loyal friend or co-worker to betray you?

 Teacher Page

The Buried Coin

The Situation

In the middle of the night, someone digs up a grave in a cemetery. The caretaker of the cemetery lives nearby and hears the noise. The thief is surprised and runs away, not realizing he has dropped a coin that was worth $7 million. How did the coin get there?

The Clues

1. The man buried in the grave was John Leigh, an unemployed taxi driver.	2. John Leigh died of pneumonia in room 209 at City Hospital nine days before.
3. The coin was owned by billionaire Frank X. Williamson, who died in a car crash not long ago.	4. Frank bought the rare coin at an auction many years ago. He called it his lucky coin and kept it with him at all times.
5. His only child, Lucy, came to City Hospital as soon as she heard about the crash. Unfortunately, he had already died by then.	6. Lucy checked the pocket where he kept his coin as soon as she arrived. The coin was missing.
7. Police searched the room (207), the car, and even the people who had been in the room. They found nothing.	8. His chauffeur, who had only minor injuries, was allowed to stay in Frank's hospital room. He was the first to hear the doctors say Frank would not survive.
9. The doctors called Lucy right after speaking to the chauffeur.	

The Third Man

The Situation

A night cleaner at an office building hears a noise in the basement. He goes to investigate and sees two men: one in a suit and one in jeans and a T-shirt (the "third man"). They are both carrying briefcases. The man in the suit tells the other man, "When he gets here, we each give him half the money." Suddenly, a police officer comes in. The policeman and the man in the suit shoot each other. The third man runs off.

The cleaner runs to call police and goes back to the basement. When he gets back, there is nothing there: no bodies, no blood, and no sign of anything having happened. What happened?

Hints

1. Was the police officer who was shot really a police officer?
2. Why couldn't police find any sign of a double murder?
3. Did the partner and the fake police officer know each other?
4. What happened to the money that the third man brought to the crime scene?

The Solution

The whole situation was a con. The partner and the fake police officer were working together to steal $50,000 from the third man. They invented the story about the diamond smuggler, led him to an empty basement and staged a double murder. They knew the man wouldn't go to police to confess his involvement in buying diamonds illegally. When the third man ran away, the other two took his briefcase with the money.

Follow-Up Question

This is a trick to steal money from people. It is featured in a lot of movies and books and TV shows. Can you think of any other well-known ways to trick people out of money?

 Teacher Page

The Third Man

<table>
<tr><td>

The Situation

    A night cleaner at an office building hears a noise in the basement. He goes to investigate and sees two men: one in a suit and one in jeans and a T-shirt (the "third man"). They are both carrying briefcases. The man in the suit tells the other man, "When he gets here, we each give him half the money." Suddenly, a police officer comes in. The policeman and the man in the suit shoot each other. The third man runs off.

The cleaner runs to call police and goes back to the basement. When he gets back, there is nothing there: no bodies, no blood, and no sign of anything having happened. What happened?

</td></tr>
</table>

The Clues

1. The only thing out of place was that the basement door had been forced open from the outside.	2. Police showed no reports of an officer in that area, and no policemen were wounded or missing that night.
3. By talking to witnesses who saw him running, police were able to trace the third man to his home.	4. He told police he had met the man in the suit a few weeks ago who offered to partner with him to buy illegal diamonds for a low price and sell them later.
5. Both the third man and the man in the suit were putting in $50,000 each to buy the diamonds.	6. The two men exchanged briefcases to check that the money was correct. At that moment a policeman entered the basement.
7. The third man said that, after the shooting, he ran with the other man's briefcase.	8. When he opened the briefcase, it was full of worthless paper.
9. He told police that he didn't report the murder because he didn't want to be arrested for diamond smuggling.	10. The police found a police uniform, a suit, and an empty briefcase in a garbage can near the train station. There were no signs of blood on anything.

Your student detectives might also be interested in

Verdicts

Real Court Cases to Argue and Resolve

Here is a sample case. Other samples at ProLinguaAssociates.com.

13 ❋ The Unlucky Poodle

(Arizona)

Marjorie was taking her poodle for its daily walk around the neighborhood near her home. She was very fond of her dog and cared for it with devotion, taking it out every day for exercise and just for fun.

But this day was different—in a bad way. A large St. Bernard attacked her little dog, severely injuring him. In fact, the St. Bernard bit off one of the poodle's legs, and Marjorie's dog died just two days later. The vet could not save it. Marjorie, of course, was heartbroken.

She sued the owner of the St. Bernard for damages. She was suffering, she said, from great emotional shock and distress from witnessing the scary incident. This emotional suffering had caused her to seek medical help. Furthermore, she had felt endangered herself from the St. Bernard, although the dog did not harm her or even threaten her during the incident.

Did Marjorie get damages for her emotional distress during and after this disturbing event? Was she awarded anything for the loss of her beloved pet?

---

13 ❋ The Unlucky Poodle *(Pages 36-37)*

The court did not give the poodle owner any damages. She lost the case. The court said that a dog is personal property, not in the same category as a relative or close friend. Witnessing injury to property is not a valid reason for an award of emotional distress. A dog is not the same as a person.

Copyright © 2016 by John Miller and Raymond Clark • Photocopyable